Popular Culture:

1920–1939

Jane Bingham

www.raintreepublishers.co.uk
Visit our website to find out more information about Raintree books.

To order:
☎ Phone 0845 6044371
🖷 Fax +44 (0) 1865 312263
🖳 Email myorders@raintreepublishers.co.uk

Customers from outside the UK please telephone +44 1865 312262

Raintree is an imprint of Capstone Global Library Limited, a company incorporated in England and Wales having its registered office at 7 Pilgrim Street, London, EC4V 6LB – Registered company number: 6695582

Edited by Adam Miller, Andrew Farrow, and
  Adrian Vigliano
Designed by Richard Parker
Original illustrations © Capstone Global Ltd 2013
Illustrations by Richard Parker
Picture research by Mica Brancic
Originated by Capstone Global Library Ltd
Printed and bound in China by Leo Paper Products Ltd

ISBN 978 1 406 24021 4
16 15 14 13 12
10 9 8 7 6 5 4 3 2 1

British Library Cataloguing in Publication Data
TO COME
A full catalogue record for this book is available from the British Library.

Acknowledgements
We would like to thank the following for permission to reproduce photographs: Corbis pp. 14, 47 (© Bettmann), 39 (Reuters/© Luke MacGregor); Getty Images pp. 4 (Central Press), 5 (Time Life Pictures/ Margaret Bourke-White), 7 (Dorothea Lange), 9, 12, 15, 18 (Redferns/Gilles Petard), 11 (Frank Driggs Collection), 13 (NY Daily News Archive), 16, 19, 21, 29 (Moviepix/John Kobal Foundation),17 (Moviepix/Warner Brothers), 23 (Moviepix/Warner Bros./Chaplin- First National), 25 (Hulton Archive/ Moveipix/Paramount Pictures), 27 (Time Life Pictures/Buyenlarge), 30 (Hulton Archive/Moviepix/Silver Screen Collection), 32 (Hulton Archive/Fox Photos/ Richards), 35 (Popperfoto), 38 (Hulton Archive/ Moviepix), 40, 48 (New York Daily News Archive/ New York Daily News), 43 (Hulton Archive/General Photographic Agency), 44 (Archive Photos/American Stock Archive), 49 (Archive Photos/New York Times Co.), 50 (Hulton ArchivePuttnam/Topical Press Agency), 53 (Archive Photos/Chicago History Museum); Library of Congress p. 41 (Historic American Buildings Survey); Photoshot pp. 37, 51 (© UPPA). Background images and design features reproduced with permission of Shutterstock.

Cover photograph of American blues singer Mamie Smith reproduced with the permission of Getty Images (Frank Driggs Collection).

Contents

Some words are printed in bold, **like this**. You can find out what they mean by looking in the glossary.

What is popular culture?

This book looks at popular culture between the years 1920 and 1939. It shows how ordinary people liked to enjoy themselves and how they spent their leisure time. In the 1920s, young people began to listen to new kinds of music and wore daring new fashions. The 1920s and 1930s were a great time for cinema and radio, and people of all ages read books, comics, and magazines. New styles of art, design, and architecture were introduced. People began to travel by motorcycle and car, and even by ship and plane, and a series of crazes swept through North America and Europe.

After World War I

In 1918, World War I came to an end, and millions of young soldiers returned home. Many of these young men found it very hard to settle back into the lives that they had known before. They realized they were lucky to be alive, and they wanted to have a good time while they were still young.

While the men had been away at war, some young women had taken over their jobs. These women had grown used to having more freedom, and they were determined not to return to the old ways. The 1920s were an especially exciting time for women. For the first time ever, a young woman could have a job, stay out late, and even drive a car.

In the 1920s, many people just wanted to have fun. This couple is dancing the Charleston, a popular dance of the period.

Youth culture is born

There was a sense of rebellion among many young people in the 1920s. This spirit was expressed in a culture that was very different from that of the older generation. The 1920s saw the birth of a "youth culture", with young people wearing different clothes, listening to different music, and enjoying different dances to their parents.

The Roaring Twenties

In the 10 years following World War I, the **economy** boomed, especially in the United States. There was a growing demand for **consumer goods**, and people had more money to spend on enjoying themselves. The 1920s are sometimes known as the Roaring Twenties because some businesses roared ahead, and some fortunate people had a roaring good time!

Even though alcohol was officially banned in the United States between 1920 and 1933, people still gathered at speakeasies, such as this bar in New York.

Prohibition and speakeasies

In 1920, the US government decided to take action to solve the many social problems caused by alcohol. They passed a national law, known as **Prohibition**, that put a total ban on making and selling alcohol. Prohibition lasted until 1933.[1] During this period gangsters known as bootleggers smuggled alcohol into the United States, and illegal bars sprang up everywhere. The bars were known as **speakeasies** and they became very popular with young people. Jazz musicians played in the speakeasies while people drank, smoked, and danced to the music.

Life in the 1930s

During the 1930s, life became much harder for many people. In 1929, countries all over the world plunged into the **Great Depression**. This was a period of widespread poverty, when banks and businesses failed and millions of people lost their jobs. The Great Depression lasted for most of the 1930s. However, by the end of the decade, there were signs of recovery.[2]

By the late 1930s, the United States had become the dominant world economy. It also set trends in popular culture, with people all over the world listening to American jazz and watching American films.

A dangerous world

The 1930s saw a growing threat from Germany. By 1933, Adolf Hitler and his Nazi party had gained control of Germany.[3] Hitler began to make plans to create a "Greater Germany" by invading neighbouring countries. He also launched a campaign to **persecute** Jews, gypsies, and disabled people. By the late 1930s, it was clear that the only way to stop Hitler from achieving his aims was to go to war with Germany.

During the 1930s, there was also widespread fear of **communism**. By 1929, Joseph Stalin had become leader of the Soviet Union and taken total control of the Russian people's lives.[4] Many people feared that communist ideas would spread to Europe and America.

A world of entertainment

Faced with serious problems at home and abroad, many people chose to escape into the comforting world of entertainment. Cinema and radio were immensely popular, and they brought people together in a new kind of community. In particular, romantic films, such as *Gone With the Wind* and *The Wizard of Oz*, attracted massive audiences around the world. The 1930s also saw the growth of celebrity culture, as people worldwide identified with film stars, singers, and musicians.

The Great Depression hit families especially hard, as parents struggled to find enough food to feed their children.

Breaking the law

In the desperate years of the Great Depression, many people in the United States were driven to crime. Most lawbreakers stole small amounts of money to keep their families alive. However, some armed outlaws moved from town to town, breaking into shops, petrol stations, and banks. The most famous outlaws of the period were Bonnie Parker and Clyde Barrow. Bonnie and Clyde drove through Texas and the surrounding states, robbing banks as they went. Eventually, the police caught up with them and shot and killed them in 1934.[5] After they died, Bonnie and Clyde became glamorous figures in American popular culture, and were widely admired for their daring and style.

Jazz, blues, and swing

The 1920s are often known as the Jazz Age because jazz really took off in those years. The craze for jazz began in America but soon spread to Europe. People went to bars and clubs to listen to jazz musicians and singers. Fans bought **sheet music** to play at home, and millions of people bought records by stars such as Louis Armstrong and Bessie Smith.

Jazz begins

Jazz had its origins in the early years of the twentieth century. It began in New Orleans, Louisiana, where a group of talented African American musicians developed a new kind of music.[1] Their music was based on the songs their ancestors had sung when they were working as slaves on cotton plantations.

Jazz stood out from other popular music of the time because of its very strong rhythms and its use of **blues** notes (notes in a **minor key**) to create a sad and haunting mood. Jazz music was often played by a small group of musicians on a range of instruments, such as a saxophone, a trumpet, a banjo, and a piano. There were parts for solo players, who were free to **improvise** some of the music as they went along.

From New Orleans to Chicago

Most of the early jazz musicians were based in the city of New Orleans. Two leading figures in this group of musicians were Joe Oliver, often known as the King, and Jelly Roll Morton. Oliver led King Oliver's Creole Jazz Band, and Morton's band was known as the Red Hot Peppers.

In the early 1920s, musicians from New Orleans started to move to Chicago, Illinois. Oliver arrived in 1919, and he was soon joined by a young trumpeter named Louis Armstrong.[2] Morton and his band moved to Chicago in 1923.[3] Jazz musicians performed in the city's many speakeasies, and Chicago became the heart of the jazz music scene.

Louis Armstrong was nicknamed Satchmo, which is short for "satchel mouth". This was probably because he had a large mouth. He was famous for his trumpet playing and for his deep bass voice.

Louis Armstrong (1901-1971)

Louis Armstrong grew up in New Orleans, Louisiana. He came from a very poor family and was sent to a reform school at the age of 14, after firing a gun in the air. At the school he learned to play the trumpet, and when he was 16 years old he joined Joe Oliver's jazz band. Five years later, in 1922, he moved to Chicago, Illinois, to play with Oliver. In the late 1920s, he made some famous recordings with groups called Louis Armstrong's Hot Five and Hot Seven. During the 1930s, Armstrong toured all over the United States and also played in Denmark, Sweden, Norway, Holland, and England. Armstrong had a long and successful career. He made his last recording when he was 66 years old.[4]

By the mid 1920s, the jazz craze had spread across the United States and had even reached Europe. Musicians went on tour to different cities and countries, people bought sheet music and records, and many new bands were formed. New York became an exciting centre for jazz, and the singer and dancer Josephine Baker took jazz to Paris.

Jazz records had become big business in the 1920s, selling millions of copies across the world. Two of the biggest hits were Louis Armstrong's "Potato Head Blues" and "West End Blues".

Dancing the Charleston

People loved to dance to jazz. The most popular dance of the Jazz Age was the Charleston. This dance was first performed by African Americans in the city of Charleston, South Carolina. It was made popular by a tune called "The Charleston" in the hit musical *Runnin' Wild*, which ran on **Broadway**, in New York, in 1923.[5]

Dancers of the Charleston kicked their feet very fast and swung their hands backwards and forwards. Unlike many earlier, more formal dances, it could be danced alone, with a partner, or in a group. The Charleston was especially popular with young women, known as flappers, who shocked the older generation with their daring moves. Other popular dances were the black bottom and the shimmy.

Singing the blues

In the 1920s, singers of the blues became very popular. The early blues singers were African American women, who sang sad but powerful songs with a jazz rhythm. Mamie Smith made the first blues recording in 1920. It included her famous song "Crazy Blues" and sold a million copies in less than a year.[6]

Mamie Smith's hit was soon followed by records by Bessie Smith and Gertrude "Ma" Rainey. Gertrude Rainey was sometimes known as the Mother of the Blues. By 1928 she had made 90 recordings.[7] Bessie Smith was the most popular female blues singer of the 1920s and 1930s, and she toured all over the United States.[8] Her passionate and soulful style, in songs such as "Downhearted Blues", was copied by many later singers.

Quote

Many people objected to jazz in its early days. Thomas Edison, inventor of the electric lightbulb and founder of Edison Records, said that he "always played jazz backwards because it sounded better that way". He also stated that jazz was "for the nuts" and claimed that one jazz performance reminded him of "the dying moan of dead animals".[9]

Bessie Smith was sometimes called the Empress of the Blues.

Big bands

In the early 1920s, some talented jazz **soloists** started to form "big bands". These bands had up to 25 players and included wind instruments (such as saxophones, trumpets, and trombones), strings (such as guitars and a double bass), and at least one set of drums. The bands also featured a solo singer. Big bands performed in dance halls and clubs and also broadcast on the radio. They reached a peak of popularity in the 1930s.

One of the biggest radio stars of the 1930s was Earl "Fatha" Hines, whose band played in the Grand Terrace Cafe in Chicago. Duke Ellington, Benny Goodman, and Count Basie all had famous big bands. Benny Goodman was one of the first white Americans to become a big band leader.

A style called swing

Big bands played in a style called **swing**. Swing tunes were similar to jazz, but they were more structured and had fewer improvised passages. Most swing tunes had a very fast rhythm and were very easy to dance to. Bandleaders composed new tunes for their bands, but they also relied on popular numbers, which were often songs from musicals. Most of these songs were very romantic. Some big swing hits of the late 1920s and 1930s were "Anything Goes", "On the Sunny Side of the Street", and "It's Only a Paper Moon".

Duke Ellington (bottom left) got his nickname because of his elegant clothes and perfect manners.

Dance halls

Big bands often played in large dance halls, where young people gathered to listen to music and dance. Popular dances from the 1930s were the Lindy Hop, the jitterbug, and the shim sham. The Lindy Hop developed from the Charleston. It involved bending the knees and kicking the feet, but also leaping high into the air. In the jitterbug, dancers swayed their hips and twitched their arms and legs. Dancers of the shim sham shuffled their feet in a kind of tap dance.

A prize-winning dancer shows her friends and family how she won first place in a Lindy Hop competition.

Did you know?

Some male dancers of the Lindy Hop performed a move called "over the back". In this exciting move, the man threw his female partner right over his head so that she landed on the floor behind him!

Duke Ellington (1899-1974)

Duke Ellington's real name was Edward Kennedy Ellington. He grew up in a middle-class family in Washington, DC. After leaving school he trained as an artist, but he soon found full-time work as a jazz pianist. In 1923, he moved to Harlem, New York, and in the following year he became a bandleader. From 1927 to 1931, Duke Ellington was the bandleader at the Cotton Club in Harlem. His band had a weekly radio show and made many hit records. In the 1930s, he went on tour to Europe. He led his band until his death at the age of 75 and wrote over 1,000 musical compositions.[10]

The Harlem Renaissance

African Americans played a major role in the popular culture of the 1920s and 1930s. They introduced the new musical styles of jazz, blues, and swing and also had an impact in the theatre and on literature. The most important centre for black American culture in this period was the Harlem district, in New York. It was home to a cultural movement called the Harlem Renaissance.

Music in Harlem

In the 1920s and 1930s, Harlem had two world-famous music clubs. The Apollo Theater staged **variety shows** featuring black singers, dancers, and comedians. It also held amateur nights to introduce new talent. In 1934, the 17-year-old singer Ella Fitzgerald was discovered at an amateur night at the Apollo Theater.[11]

The Cotton Club was a nightclub that served alcohol illegally during the Prohibition years and was especially famous for its jazz. Duke Ellington was the Club's bandleader from 1927 to 1931, and some outstanding singers and musicians, such as Ella Fitzgerald, Billie Holiday, and Fats Waller, performed there. In the 1920s, the Cotton Club operated a strict colour bar. This meant that even though the club's owner, staff, and musicians were all African Americans, only white people were admitted as customers. In the 1930s, the colour bar rules were relaxed somewhat, as the club began to admit light-skinned non-whites.[12]

Couples dance to the music of a big band in Harlem's Cotton Club. In the 1920s, the Club only admitted white customers.

Powerful voices

In the years between World War I and World War II, a group of very talented African Americans produced books and plays, and campaigned for greater recognition for African Americans. Langston Hughes was one of the key figures of the Harlem Renaissance. He wrote novels, short stories, plays, poetry, and operas – all presenting the African American viewpoint. His play, *Mulatto: A Tragedy of the Deep South*, was performed on Broadway in 1935.[13] It revealed the sufferings of the Southern black people in the first part of the twentieth century. In 1937, Zora Neale Hurston published a best-selling novel called *Their Eyes Were Watching God*.[14] It told the story of a black community in Florida through the eyes of the women in the town.

Ella Fitzgerald had an outstanding career as a jazz singer, and became known as the "First Lady of Song".

Did you know?

In the 1930s, a cartoon character called Torchy Brown introduced Harlem to the wider world. Torchy was a teenage girl from Mississippi who travelled to Harlem, and found fame and fortune by singing and dancing in the Cotton Club. Torchy was created by Jackie Ormes, the first African American woman to work as a cartoonist.

Vaudeville, musicals, and dance

People flocked to variety shows in the 1920s. These shows were made up of a series of acts by musicians, dancers, singers, comedians, magicians, and acrobats. Variety shows had begun in the 1880s and were still extremely popular in the years after World War I. By the 1930s, however, variety shows were on their way out, as musicals and films took their place as the new forms of popular entertainment.

Vaudeville shows

Variety entertainment was known as **vaudeville** in the United States and Canada. Most vaudeville companies took their shows on tour, but some famous shows had a permanent home. In New York, the Ziegfeld Follies ran on Broadway from 1907 to 1931 and starred the biggest names in show business.[1]

US vaudeville shows often featured Jewish comedians and singers. Stars such as Fanny Brice, Sophie Tucker, and Al Jolson sang songs and told jokes about Jewish family life. There were also Italian comedians, such as Jimmy Durante, who made fun of Italian **immigrants**. Some vaudeville entertainers painted their faces black and sang **minstrel songs** (see box at right).

Many vaudeville performers later moved into cinema and radio. The early cinema stars Buster Keaton, Charlie Chaplin, and Mae West began their careers in vaudeville. The variety stars Fanny Brice and Jimmy Durante both had radio shows in the 1930s.

Buster Keaton was a star of vaudeville and cinema. He is shown here in the silent movie *Go West*, which was released in 1925.

16

Music hall

In the United Kingdom variety shows were known as music hall shows, or just music hall. Singers and comedians from the north of England, such as Gracie Fields and George Formby, were especially popular, and music hall shows also included minstrel songs. George Formby played the ukulele, which is like a small guitar, and sang **bawdy** songs. One of his best-known numbers was "When I'm Cleaning Windows", which described some of the sights that a window cleaner saw as he worked!

Al Jolson performing in blackface in the 1927 film *The Jazz Singer*.

Minstrel shows

The tradition of the black minstrel show dates back to the United States in the 1840s. Minstrel shows featured singers, dancers, and comedians in black make-up (called blackface) and white gloves, making fun of African Americans. By the 1920s, minstrel shows were no longer popular, but singers still "blacked up" and performed minstrel songs. Even in the 1950s minstrel songs were still featured in some variety shows. However, by that time, most people had realized that minstrel acts were insulting to African Americans.[2]

17

Cabarets are variety shows that are performed in nightclubs or bars. They tended to be more sophisticated than vaudeville or music hall and appealed to wealthier audiences. Cabaret shows were especially popular in France and Germany in the 1920s. In France the best-known cabaret was the Folies Bergère. It had begun in the 1860s, but was still very popular in the early twentieth century. American-born entertainer Josephine Baker was a major star of the Folies Bergère in the 1920s.

Josephine Baker was not just a cabaret artist. She also starred in several French films and became a worldwide celebrity.

Josephine Baker (1906-1975)

Josephine Baker came from a very poor family in St. Louis, Missouri, USA. At the age of eight, she was hired as a maid and had to sleep in a coal cellar. Fortunately she managed to escape from her life of poverty through her talent as a dancer and comedian. By the time she was 16 she was dancing in a touring vaudeville show. In her late teens she moved to New York, where she soon became one of the stars of Broadway vaudeville. In 1925 she moved to Paris, where she continued to perform as a singer, dancer, and entertainer. During World War II she worked as a spy for the **French resistance** movement.[3]

German cabarets were different from variety shows in other countries. Although they featured songs and comic sketches, they had a very serious aim. German cabaret performers used their songs and comic routines as a way to criticize their government. The German cabarets began in the 1900s. They were especially active during the 1930s, at the time that Adolf Hitler came to power.

Musicals take off

Musical theatre, or plays that included songs, had existed since the 1700s, but this form of entertainment was transformed after World War I. Starting around 1920, some very talented American composers began to create what came to be known as musicals. The new musicals were fast paced and exciting with glamorous costumes and settings. They included spectacular dance routines and featured some "show-stopping" songs for the star solo singers.

Some outstanding musicals from the 1920s include *Lady Be Good* by George and Ira Gershwin, *Showboat* by Jerome Kern and Oscar Hammerstein, and *No, No, Nanette* by composer Vincent Youmans, featuring the classic song "Tea for Two".

The Broadway Melody of 1929 was a very popular film about musical stars. It featured the romances of stars from a Broadway show.

Cabaret in Nazi Germany

In the early 1930s, Hitler's Nazi party became very popular in Germany. The Nazis claimed that the Jews were to blame for many of the country's problems, and they promised to make Germany the most powerful country in the world. Millions of people joined the Nazi party, but some Germans realized just how dangerous Hitler was.

Cabaret artists performed sketches and songs making fun of Hitler and the Nazis, and trying to warn people of the dangers ahead. For a few years, the cabaret performers managed to make their protest, but in 1933 Hitler became chancellor, or head of the German government. The cabarets were closed down, and most of the performers escaped to other countries.[4]

19

Stunning songs

The period between World War I and World War II was an amazing time for songwriting. In the United States, Cole Porter, Irving Berlin, and Richard Rodgers all composed songs that are still performed today. Porter and Berlin wrote both music and lyrics, while Rodgers worked with the lyricist Lorenz Hart. George and Ira Gershwin were another great songwriting team, with George writing the music and Ira writing the words. The English composer and writer Noël Coward produced many popular songs, as well as plays for the London stage. All these composers wrote songs for musicals.

George Gershwin (1898-1937)

George Gershwin was an outstanding American composer. He wrote several hit Broadway musicals, including *Lady Be Good* and *Funny Face*, and scores for Hollywood films. In 1935 he wrote a popular opera, *Porgy and Bess*, which is still often performed today. Gershwin also composed works for orchestra, which appealed to a very wide audience. His most famous orchestral work is *Rhapsody in Blue*. Gershwin died tragically young, in 1937, at the age of 38.[5]

Noël Coward (1899-1973)

Noël Coward grew up in London. He attended dance school and first appeared on the London stage when he was 12. This appearance marked the start of a long and varied career in the theatre. Coward danced, acted, and sang, and he also worked as a director. He started writing plays as a teenager and went on to write over 50 of them. Two of his most successful early plays were *Hay Fever* and *Private Lives*. Coward also composed hundreds of songs including the popular number, "Mad Dogs and Englishmen". During World War II he worked as a spy. Throughout his life he was famous for his wit and elegant sense of style.[6]

Dancing stars

Stars of vaudeville shows and musicals often had to dance as well as sing. One dancing duo stood out from all the rest. In the 1920s, Fred Astaire performed as a singer and a dancer with his sister Adele. Then, in 1933, he began to work with a new dancing partner, Ginger Rogers.

Astaire and Rogers made a winning combination. As well as being remarkable dancers, they were excellent actors, who made their dance routines feel like part of the story of the film. The couple made 10 films together, and achieved worldwide fame in hits such as *Flying Down to Rio* (1933) and *Top Hat* (1935).[7]

Ginger Rogers and Fred Astaire dancing together in the movie *Swing Time* (released in 1936). *Swing Time* featured the song "The Way You Look Tonight", which became a hit record for Fred Astaire.

Did you know?

According to a Hollywood legend, Fred Astaire nearly failed a screen test. Screen tests were made to determine if a person would look good in films. Apparently the report on the test said simply, "Can't sing. Can't act. Balding. Can dance a little."[8]

Fantastic films

Cinema began in the 1890s, when the first moving pictures were shown.[1] People flocked to cinemas, known as movie houses in the United States, to see silent films. The films were accompanied by music, which was played on a piano or an organ, or even by a full orchestra.

Stars of the silent screen

Silent film actors used exaggerated facial expressions so that audiences could understand exactly what they were feeling. Male stars of silent romantic films, such as Rudolph Valentino and Douglas Fairbanks, were dashing and handsome. Some female stars, such as Mary Pickford and Lillian Gish, looked sweet and innocent. Clara Bow played more daring roles, and had a major hit in 1927 with the film *It* (see page 45).

Silent comedies

Comedy films were very popular in the 1920s. Most of them were action-packed and relied on slapstick effects, such as characters falling over or bumping into things. The Keystone Kops films, starring Fatty Arbuckle, were classic slapstick comedies. They featured a set of useless policemen who chased after clever crooks.

The comic star Buster Keaton was an expert at slapstick. He could perform incredible falls without getting hurt. He also had a very expressive face, with large, deep-set eyes. One critic wrote, "with merely a stare [Buster Keaton] can convey a wide range of emotions, from longing to mistrust, from puzzlement to sorrow".[2]

Films around the world

During the 1920s, studios in France, Germany, and the Soviet Union created some outstanding silent films. French films from this period include *Nana* (directed by Jean Renoir), *Les Misérables*, and *Napoleon*. German studios produced some exceptional early horror movies, such as *Nosferatu* (1922). In 1925, the Russian director Sergei Eisenstein created *Battleship Potemkin*, a dramatic portrait of a bloody uprising surrounding a battleship belonging to the Tsar.[3]

Charlie Chaplin (1889-1977)

Charlie Chaplin was an outstanding star of the silent screen who made great use of facial expressions and body language. He was especially famous for his cheerful walk, with his knees bent and his toes turned out, and one hand twirling a cane.

Chaplin often played the character of the Little Tramp, who was very poor but who always tried to behave with dignity. One of Chaplin's best-known silent films is *The Kid*, which was **released** in 1921.[4] It features Chaplin as the Little Tramp and child actor Jackie Coogan as his adopted son and partner in crime.

The Kid combined comedy and drama, and was advertised as "A picture with a smile – and perhaps, a tear".

Did you know?

In Japan silent films had a narrator, called a *benshi*. The *benshi* stood beside the screen and told the story of the film, using a range of voices for the different characters. *Benshis* continued to work in Japanese cinema until the mid 1930s, long after the **talkies** had replaced silent films in other countries. The *benshi* provided a useful translation for western films, which were played in Japan without their soundtrack.[5]

The talkies arrive

The first film with sound was *The Jazz Singer*. It was released in 1927 and starred Al Jolson as a young Jewish boy who breaks with family tradition to become a jazz singer. Most of the film was silent, but some scenes had sound and Jolson sang six songs. Each of the songs was mounted on a separate reel of film with a separate accompanying sound disk. Even though the film was only 90 minutes long, there were 15 film reels and 15 sound disks to manage.[6]

The *Jazz Singer* was a huge success. During the first showing, the audience applauded after every song. By the end of 1929, almost all Hollywood films were talkies.

Comedy classics

Some all-time favourite comedy stars made their names in the films of the 1930s. The Marx Brothers made 10 comedy films that became comedy classics between 1929 and 1939.[7] They developed a zany comedy style in which each brother had his own distinctive personality. Groucho wore a large moustache and smoked a cigar. Chico had a fake Italian accent. Harpo never spoke. He wore a blonde curly wig and sometimes carried a taxi cab horn. Zeppo was the straight man and sometimes the romantic lead.

Stan Laurel and Oliver Hardy began their careers as silent comedy stars. They played two dim-witted but optimistic characters who struggled to achieve even the simplest tasks. Laurel and Hardy films involve slapstick routines and cartoon-like violence. Much of their comedy comes from the physical contrast between the tiny Laurel and the very large Hardy.

Modern Times

Charlie Chaplin made some classic films in the 1930s. *Modern Times*, which was released in 1936,[8] is generally considered to be his greatest achievement. It shows Chaplin as the Little Tramp struggling to survive in the modern world. In one of the film's most famous scenes, Chaplin gets stuck on a factory **assembly line**. The film is a comedy, but it is also a deliberate attack on what it sees as the inhumane nature of modern society.

The four Marx Brothers starring in their film *Duck Soup*. They are, from left to right: Chico, Zeppo, Groucho, and Harpo.

Hollywood

In the early years of the twentieth century, most American films were made in the New York area. In 1911, the first film studio was opened in Hollywood, a village close to the city of Los Angeles, California.[9] Filmmakers liked to work in California because of the state's sunny weather and its dramatic scenery, and Hollywood soon became the centre of the US film industry.

During the 1920s, five major film companies – Paramount, Warner Brothers, Columbia, MGM (Metro-Goldwyn-Mayer), and RKO (Radio-Keith-Orpheum) – established their headquarters in Hollywood. Independent studios also came to Hollywood, and film stars built large houses in the surrounding hills. By 1930, there were 20 Hollywood studios, and around 800 films were released every year.[10]

Screwball comedies

A new kind of comic film emerged in the 1930s. Screwball comedies have witty **dialogue** and fast-paced plots with many comical misunderstandings. They usually involve a battle between the sexes, with a strong-minded woman standing up for herself, and they often end in romance. One of the greatest screwball hits of the 1930s was *It Happened One Night*. It starred Claudette Colbert as a socialite on the run and Clark Gable as the wisecracking reporter she meets along the way.

Horror movies

The first horror movies were silent films. *The Cabinet of Dr. Caligari*, released in 1920, has been described as the "granddaddy of all horror films".[11] It features an evil doctor who captures an innocent victim. In 1922, *Nosferatu* became the first vampire movie.[12]

In the 1930s, sound added a new element to horror films. Audiences were terrified by grunts and howls from the monsters and screams from their victims. Two classic horror films, *Dracula* and *Frankenstein*, were released in 1931. *Frankenstein* proved so popular that a **sequel** was made in 1935, called *The Bride of Frankenstein*.[13]

King Kong

In 1933, RKO studios released *King Kong*, a film that combined horror with adventure.[14] *King Kong* tells the story of a monstrous, giant gorilla who is taken from his tropical home on Skull Island to New York City. In the film's climactic scene the monster climbs the Empire State Building, clutching the heroine in one enormous hand. At the very last moment, a courageous pilot rescues the heroine and topples the monster, who falls to his death. The heroine was played by Fay Wray, who specialized in horror movies and became known as the "scream queen".

King Kong set a new record for audience numbers. People loved the story of a modern-day beauty and the beast, and they were amazed by the film's **special effects**.

The dramatic poster for the movie *King Kong* featured the monster perched on the top of the Empire State Building.

SPECIAL EFFECTS

Four models were made to represent the monster in *King Kong*. The models were filmed using a technique called stop-motion, in which a model is moved a tiny amount at a time and filmed each time in a slightly different position. Then all the shots are put together to make it look as if the model is moving smoothly.

Two jointed models measuring 45 centimetres (18 inches) high were used for the Skull Island scenes. One jointed model measuring 60 centimetres (24 inches) was used for the action in New York. A fourth small model made from lead and fur was used to represent King Kong in his final fall from the top of the Empire State Building. For the three jointed models, King Kong's body was made of light aluminium covered with rabbit fur. His lips, eyebrows, and nose were made from rubber and his eyes were made from glass. The monster's facial expressions were controlled by thin, bendable wires threaded through holes drilled in his skull.[15]

Action and adventure

Action and adventure films were very popular in the 1930s. Some told exciting stories with a historical background, such as *The Adventures of Robin Hood* and *Mutiny on the Bounty*. Some featured pirates or bandits, such as *Captain Blood* and *Stingaree*, and some were set in remote islands or jungles, such as *Tarzan the Ape Man*. Most adventure films had a strong **moral** message: heroes fought to save innocent lives and villains were punished for their evil deeds.

Gangster movies

Some film directors in the 1930s aimed to create more realistic films. The rise of the gangster movie reflected the rise in crime during the period of Prohibition and the Great Depression. *Little Caesar*, released in 1930, featured a gangland boss, played by Edward G. Robinson.[16] In 1931, a film called *The Public Enemy* starred James Cagney as a defiant urban gangster.[17] Following the success of these two films, Robinson and Cagney starred in a series of gritty gangster movies throughout the 1930s.

Gangster movies included dramatic shoot-'em-up scenes. These were filmed using guns that fired real bullets, because the special effects had not yet been developed to show holes put in cars or chips flying off walls. Experts would stand behind the film cameras and fire their guns near the actors. James Cagney was one of the first stars to refuse to appear in movie scenes where live bullets were used.[18]

Early westerns

As early as 1920, westerns had proved to be a financial success. They were cheap to make **on location** in California or Nevada, and there were endless ways to present the basic plot of a battle between the "good-guy" cowboys and the "bad-guy" Indians. The biggest star of the silent westerns was William S. Hart, who worked as an actor and a director.

In the 1930s, studios began to produce shorter and more light-hearted westerns, in which the heroes sang country-and-western songs. These low-budget movies were known as singing cowboy films. Gene Autry, Roy Rogers, and William Boyd (better known as Hopalong Cassidy) were all popular singing cowboys.

FILMING IN TECHNICOLOR

In 1922, a company called Technicolor began to experiment with different ways of creating coloured film. None of their methods were completely successful until 1932. Then Technicolor launched a new kind of film, made by a process called 3-strip colour. This new kind of film was often referred to as "glorious Technicolor" and it produced very vivid colours. The first full-length film it was used in was *Becky Sharp* in 1935.[19]

A scene from the gangster movie *Scarface*, released in 1932. *Scarface* tells the story of a violent power struggle in a Chicago gang.

Musical films

After the introduction of sound in 1927, many musical films were produced, but the public soon turned to more exciting movies. However, there was a great revival in musical films in 1933. In this year, Fred Astaire and Ginger Rogers made their first film together, *Flying Down to Rio*.[20] Also in 1933, the director Busby Berkeley launched two musicals, *42nd Street* and *Gold Diggers of 1933*.[21] Berkeley created spectacular dance routines, involving human bodies forming patterns like a kaleidoscope. The musicals of the 1930s were very glamorous. They appealed to people who wanted to forget the troubles of the Great Depression.

A scene from *The Wizard of Oz*, showing from left to right: the Tin Man, the Cowardly Lion, Dorothy, the doorman to the Emerald City, and the Scarecrow.

Stars of the 1930s

Film stars of the 1930s included Katharine Hepburn, Bette Davis, and Jean Harlow. They starred with male leads such as Clark Gable, Jimmy Stewart, and Cary Grant. All these actors looked very glamorous, but they also had excellent acting skills. Several child actors emerged in these years, including Judy Garland, Shirley Temple, and Jackie Cooper.

In the 1930s, foreign stars began to arrive in Hollywood. They included Greta Garbo from Sweden and Marlene Dietrich from Germany. Garbo and Dietrich were greatly admired for their elegant and sophisticated style, which was copied by many women. The English actress Vivien Leigh had a huge success playing Scarlett O'Hara in *Gone With the Wind*.

Disney cartoons

Walt Disney was a talented artist who taught himself to create **animated** cartoons. This technique involves making thousands of drawings that are each filmed separately, before the shots are put together to create a moving image (similar to a flip book). Disney began making animated films in 1923. Over the next four years he created the *Alice Comedies*, 56 short films that showed a real little girl having adventures in a cartoon world.[22]

In 1928, Disney created a cartoon character called Mickey Mouse. The first film starring Mickey Mouse was *Steamboat Willie*, and it was an instant success. Mickey was soon followed by the cartoon characters of Pluto, Goofy, and Donald Duck. In 1937, Disney produced *Snow White and the Seven Dwarfs*, the first full-length animated film.[23]

1939: The year of the blockbusters[24]

Films released in 1939, an outstanding year for the movie industry, included:

Gone With the Wind (starring Vivien Leigh and Clark Gable)
Goodbye, Mr. Chips (a British film, starring Robert Donat)
Mr. Smith Goes to Washington (starring Jimmy Stewart)
Of Mice and Men (based on a book by John Steinbeck, written in 1937)
Stagecoach (starring John Wayne in his first major role)
The Wizard of Oz (starring Judy Garland)
Wuthering Heights (starring Laurence Olivier)

The Golden Age of Radio

The years between World War I and World War II were the Golden Age of Radio. The first commercial radio station in the United States was set up in 1920, and within two years regular entertainment programmes were being broadcast across the states.[1] In the United Kingdom, the British Broadcasting Corporation (BBC) began broadcasting in 1922.[2] By the mid 1920s, most countries in the developed world had their own radio stations. Families saved up to buy a radio, which they listened to every day.

A range of programmes

Radio stations broadcast a wide range of information, music, entertainment, and educational programmes. Every day there were regular news bulletins, commentary on the events of the day, weather forecasts, and reports on sporting events. Drama was an important element of early radio, with people tuning in to hear regular **serials**. Adventure, comedy, horror, mystery, and romance were all represented in plays and serials. To please more serious listeners, there were talks by experts on their special subjects. There were also many lively quiz shows and talent shows.

In the 1930s, listening to the radio was an important part of family life. Families gathered together to listen to news bulletins, sports reports, concerts, and shows.

All kinds of music

A lot of radio air time was devoted to broadcasting music. In the 1920s, music made up three-quarters of the total programmes of the BBC.[3] The radio-listening public could enjoy a wide range of music, both classical and popular. From the earliest days of radio, performances of classical concerts and operas were broadcast live from major concert halls. In the 1930s, national radio stations, such as the National Broadcasting Company (NBC) in the United States and the BBC in Britain, formed their own orchestras, which performed on the radio many times each week.[4]

Dance bands had regular radio spots. In the United Kingdom, the Savoy Orpheans played from the Savoy Hotel in London. In the United States, Earl Hines broadcast live on coast-to-coast radio from the Grand Terrace Cafe in Chicago. These hugely popular dance bands played all the latest jazz and swing numbers, and had an important role in spreading the craze for jazz in the 1920s.

Other types of music were not forgotten. Tunes by military marching bands were popular in the United Kingdom. In the United States, country-and-western music was broadcast widely. In 1927, a weekly programme called *Grand Ole Opry* started broadcasting from Nashville, Tennessee, the home of country music.[5]

Quote

In the early 1920s, live broadcasts on the BBC often had breaks between musical pieces or news reports. During these breaks the radio went silent. One listener wrote to say how much she liked the silences:

"You will be pleased to hear how much I have enjoyed your news of the air race. I have enjoyed equally the three-minute intervals, which have given me time to reach the kitchen and baste the joint for dinner."[6]

Comedy

Radio stations ran regular comedy shows. *The Rise of the Goldbergs* was a huge success in the United States, running from 1929 to 1945.[7] It featured an immigrant family trying to come to terms with the American way of life, and starred Gertrude Berg as the mother, Molly Goldberg, and Fanny Brice as her terrible toddler, Baby Snooks. The British comedy programme *Band Waggon* presented a couple of friends, played by Arthur Askey and Richard Murdoch, who shared a flat with a goat and four pigeons. Comedy shows such as *The Rise of the Goldbergs* and *Band Waggon* introduced catchphrases that were repeated in every programme. For example, Molly Goldberg's catchphrase was "Yoo-hoo, Mrs Bloom!" The programmes were often recorded in front of a studio audience who laughed loudly at all the jokes.

Drama

By the mid-1920s, writers were creating plays for radio. In 1938, the actor Orson Welles (see photo on right) presented a radio play based on a science fiction novel, *The War of the Worlds*. The play began with a series of radio news bulletins, in which an announcer warned that the world was being attacked by aliens. The play was so realistic that hundreds of people panicked and rushed into the street to look up at the sky for aliens.[8]

Some radio dramas were presented as weekly serials. Each **episode** ended in a dramatic cliff-hanger to make sure listeners tuned in again the following week.

Children's Hour

In 1922, the BBC launched a programme called *Children's Hour*. The programme was presented by a group of friendly adults, known as Uncles and Aunts. Some exciting experiments were tried out on *Children's Hour*. The first play written for radio, the first story to be read aloud on the air, and the first broadcast of the sounds of zoo animals were all featured on *Children's Hour*.

Television begins

The first TV programmes were broadcast in the 1930s. From 1936 to 1939, the BBC broadcast TV for an average of four hours a day, while TV broadcasting began in the United States in 1938. Early TV programmes included animated cartoons, concerts, and speeches from politicians. However, the picture quality was very bad, so most people preferred to listen to the radio. The outbreak of World War II, in 1939, put an end to most experiments with TV broadcasting.[10]

The actor Orson Welles in the CBS studio, broadcasting *The War of the Worlds*. He later broadcast an apology for the panic he had caused.

Did you know?

In the 1920s, the BBC started to broadcast royal speeches. The first king's speech was given by King George V in 1924. His speech was broadcast through giant loudspeakers placed outside some major London **department stores**. The crowds around the speakers were so large that they stopped traffic in the streets.[11]

Books, magazines, and comics

The 1920s and 1930s were great years for writers. Some outstanding authors of the age include F. Scott Fitzgerald, Ernest Hemingway, William Faulkner, T. S. Eliot, James Joyce, D. H. Lawrence, George Orwell, and Graham Greene. Some of these classic authors also appealed to popular tastes and became best sellers.

American best sellers

The biggest best seller of the period was Margaret Mitchell's romantic novel *Gone With the Wind*. It was set at the time of the American Civil War, and focused on the story of Scarlett O'Hara, the spoiled daughter of a cotton plantation owner. *Gone With the Wind* was published in 1936. Within six months, it had sold a million copies.[1] In 1939, the book was made into one of the most popular films in the history of Hollywood.

Two other hugely successful American novels were F. Scott Fitzgerald's *The Great Gatsby*, published in 1925, and John Steinbeck's *The Grapes of Wrath*, published in 1939. *The Great Gatsby* captures the mood of the young and wealthy during the Roaring Twenties. *The Grapes of Wrath* is set during the harshest years of the Great Depression.

British best sellers

In the United Kingdom, two best sellers of 1938 reflected very different aspects of British life. Graham Greene's *Brighton Rock* reveals the sordid world of criminal gangs. Daphne du Maurier's *Rebecca* is a romantic story of passion and revenge, set in a beautiful country estate. The comic writer P. G. Wodehouse wrote novels and short stories reflecting the life of the English upper classes. They follow the adventures of Bertie Wooster, a lovable but stupid **aristocrat**, who is always rescued by his clever **butler**, Jeeves.

Detective stories

Stories of crime and detectives were hugely popular in the 1920s and 1930s. US crime writers produced many books with violent stories and tough detectives. In 1930, Dashiell Hammett published *The Maltese Falcon*, about a detective named Sam Spade. This was the first in a series of detective stories. Raymond Chandler also wrote tough crime fiction. In 1939, he published *The Big Sleep*, introducing his famous private detective, Philip Marlowe.

The British writer Agatha Christie wrote 80 detective mysteries, mostly set in villages or grand country houses. Some of her novels feature a Belgian detective, named Hercule Poirot. Others star Miss Marple, an eccentric English lady. Dorothy L. Sayers was another leading British crime writer. Her detective was a clever aristocrat named Lord Peter Wimsey.

The film of *Gone with the Wind* starred Clark Gable as the dashing but dangerous Rhett Butler and Vivien Leigh as the beautiful and headstrong Scarlett O'Hara.

Did you know?

In 1935, a man called Allen Lane tried to buy a good book to read on the train, but there was nothing at a reasonable price. So he decided to create a new publishing company. The company was called Penguin and it sold high-quality books in paperback. The first Penguin paperbacks included works by Ernest Hemingway and Agatha Christie. Penguin books cost very little, the equivalent of £1.00 today. The paperback revolution had begun. Today, Penguin is still one of the most respected names in publishing.[2]

Magazines

Magazines were enormously popular in the years between World War I and World War II. The 1920s saw the birth of the fan magazine and the health and fitness magazine. Celebrity magazines such as *Movie Mirror* reported on the love lives of Hollywood stars, although many of their stories were invented.

Some of the most widely read magazines were the pulps. These were collections of short stories printed on very cheap paper made from wood pulp. There were pulps for romance, horror, mystery, and crime. In 1926, a pulp magazine called *Amazing Stories* was launched to publish fantasy tales about the future. This was followed in 1930 by *Astounding Stories*. These two magazines marked the popularization of modern science fiction.[3]

Comic strips and comic books

In the 1920s, comic strips in newspapers expanded beyond humorous cartoons to include action and adventure stories. Sometimes they contained powerful political and social commentary. *Little Orphan Annie* dealt with serious themes such as the Great Depression, gangsters, and the threat of communism. *Buck Rogers* was a comic strip about a science fiction hero who represented the forces of good and fought endless battles against evil villains. *Popeye the Sailor* appealed to people who were suffering hardships during the Great Depression. Just by eating spinach Popeye could gain superhuman strength to overcome any difficulty, and even though he was poor and uneducated, he refused to be belittled by anyone.

In 1933, comic strips began to be collected into comic books. Within a few years artists were supplying new material for comic books. In 1938, *Action Comics 1* included the first appearance of Superman.[4] The character was an instant hit with readers of all ages.

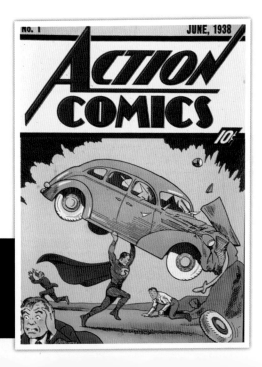

The very first image of Superman was on the cover of *Action Comics* in 1938. He was already wearing his trademark red and blue outfit.

Children's comics and comic books

In Britain, publishers produced comics for children. These were collections of comic strip stories printed on cheap paper, like a small-scale newspaper. The most famous comics of the 1930s were *The Beano* and *The Dandy*. Each year the best stories from each comic were published in an annual.

In 1929, the Belgian artist Hergé created a cartoon strip about the adventures of Tintin, a young news reporter. The cartoon was first published as a children's **supplement**, which was sold with an adult newspaper. Tintin's adventures were so popular that they were made into a series of comic books.[5]

Children's books

These classic children's books were all very popular in the 1920s and 1930s. Most of them were followed by many more works by the same author.

> *Winnie-the-Pooh* by A. A. Milne (1926)
> *Babar the Elephant* by Jean de Brunhoff (1931)
> *Mary Poppins* by P. L. Travers (1934)
> *Little House on the Prairie* by Laura Ingalls Wilder (1935)
> *The Hobbit* by J. R. R. Tolkien (1937)
> *The Sword in the Stone* by T. H. White (1938)

An employee at an auction shows the first American edition of A. A. Milne's second book about Winnie-the-Pooh, *The House at Pooh Corner* (1928).

Architecture, design, and the visual arts

In the Roaring Twenties the construction business boomed in towns and cities. Architects designed soaring skyscrapers, grand public meeting halls, theatres and cinemas, and massive factories and power stations. The Great Depression of the 1930s put a stop to these big construction projects, but house building continued throughout the 1930s. Both large and small buildings were designed in the **art deco** style.

Stunning skyscrapers

Some of the world's most famous skyscrapers were built in the 1920s. Architects had started building high at the end of the nineteenth century, but in the 1920s they became more confident and began to build much higher than before. The Chrysler Building in New York was built between 1928 and 1930.[1] It is a stunning example of the art deco style, with its shell-shaped roof pierced by triangular windows and its soaring spire. The Chrysler building was the world's tallest building until 1931, when the Empire State Building was completed.[2] It was also built in the art deco style, with blocks of decreasing size topped by a delicate mast.

The Chrysler Building and the Empire State Building still dominate the New York City skyline today.

The family homes of the 1920s and 1930s were much smaller than homes had been before. Most middle-class families no longer had live-in servants because the women and men who had previously worked as servants now chose to work in factories and shops.

In the United Kingdom, semi-detached homes became popular. These were pairs of identical houses built side-by-side as a single unit. Family homes often had stained glass in their front doors and upper windows, featuring art deco designs. The **mock-Tudor** style was widespread, and was used especially for semi-detached houses in the suburbs (on the outer edges of towns and cities).

Art moderne style architecture was one popular form in the 1930s. This is an art moderne house in Miami, Florida.

Art deco

Art deco began in Paris in the early 1920s and soon became a popular international style, lasting until the beginning of World War II. It influenced many areas of design, including architecture, furniture, and jewellery. Art deco designs have sharp, clear outlines and are symmetrical, or balanced. They use geometric shapes, such as diamonds and triangles. Typical art deco designs feature stylized plants and flowers, shells, and sunbursts. Some designs include human figures and images from modern life, such as aeroplanes, ships, and cars. The art deco style was strongly influenced by Egyptian art, which was very popular in the 1920s and 1930s.[3]

Design in the home

By the 1920s, design had become important in everyday life. Radios, **gramophones**, furniture, and lamp stands were all designed to look stylish and modern. People began to pay more attention to interior decoration, such as carpets, curtains, and wallpaper. Even bathrooms gained a modern look, with shiny tiles and mirrors. Designers made clever use of **chrome** and glass to copy the glamour of Hollywood. Cocktail cabinets, made from highly polished wood, were very fashionable, and people used lamps and mirrors to create romantic lighting effects.

Painting

The period between World War I and World War II was an exciting time for art. In the United States, Georgia O'Keeffe painted dramatic close-ups of flowers, while Edward Hopper produced bleak images of the loneliness of American life in small hotels and diners. The art style of **surrealism** was born in Europe in the 1920s, with artists such as Salvador Dalí and René Magritte creating disturbing, dreamlike images.

Two artists who appealed to the taste of the wider public were Maxfield Parrish and Mabel Lucie Attwell. Parrish was a US illustrator and painter, who began his career by illustrating magazines and children's books and producing advertising posters. He is famous for his fairy-tale style and luminous colours. Attwell created cute drawings of chubby, rosy-cheeked children. Her drawings were turned into postcards, advertisements, posters, books, and even pottery figures. She is best known for her illustrations in the book *Peter Pan*, by J. M. Barrie.

Photography

Some outstanding photographers worked in the 1920s and 1930s. Edward Weston created dramatic studies of nudes and landscapes, and Ansel Adams captured the romance of the American landscape. Dorothea Lange and Walker Evans recorded the sufferings of homeless families in the American Midwest during the Great Depression. Lange and Evans were sponsored by President Franklin Roosevelt's New Deal programme to create new work opportunities for Americans.

Exotic style

In the 1920s, people in Europe and the United States began to be more aware of the wider world. France, Germany, and Italy all had **colonies** in Africa and Asia, while the British Empire covered large areas of Africa and India. People returned to Europe from distant parts of the Empire with **exotic** treasures and exciting stories. At the same time, Hollywood films set on islands or in jungles sparked enormous interest in foreign lands. Fabrics, sculptures, and animal skins were imported in large quantities, along with raw materials such as ivory, mother-of-pearl, and tortoiseshell. For the very wealthy, it was the height of fashion to go off on safari to hunt wild animals and bring home a tiger skin. Even the less wealthy tried to have something exotic in their homes.

This room was designed in the art deco style for a 1929 film.

Did you know?

In 1922, the **archaeologist** Howard Carter discovered the tomb of the ancient Egyptian king Tutankhamen. Treasures from Tutankhamen's tomb were put on display in Europe and the United States, and the public went wild for anything connected with ancient Egypt. This passion for Egyptian art was known as Egyptomania.[*]

Fashions, stunts, and crazes

During the Roaring Twenties, there was a sense of rebellion among the younger generation. Young men and women wore daring new fashions that made them look very different to their parents. Some of them smoked and drank heavily. They stayed out late in clubs and bars listening to jazz and dancing.

Flapper style

Young women who dressed in the latest fashions and enjoyed a fast, daring lifestyle were called "flappers" and "it girls". In many people's view they showed a shocking amount of leg compared to pre-war and Victorian fashions. Flapper dresses and skirts stopped just below the knee. Dresses were shaped like a tube, with a low waist. Skirts had pleats, gathers, or slits to allow more freedom of movement. Flapper dresses were often decorated with fringes. Scarves and long strings of beads were very popular. Shoes had low heels so their wearers could dance easily.

A flapper of the 1920s demonstrating the latest style: a knee-length, low-waisted dress and a soft cloche hat.

Flappers wore comfortable underwear that allowed them to move freely. Instead of the corsets and long bloomers worn by their mothers, they wore a loose, all-in-one garment called a step-in. Some young women wound strips of cloth around the bust to make themselves look less buxom. It was fashionable to have a slim, boyish figure.

Short hair and make-up

Flappers had their hair cut short in a bob that ended at chin level. This haircut was seen as extremely shocking in the 1920s, when all young ladies were expected to have beautiful long hair. The bob was later replaced by an even shorter haircut, known as a shingle cut or Eton crop. The shingle cut was slicked down and had a curl on each cheek. Flappers often added a felt, bell-shaped hat called a cloche. They also shocked the older generation by wearing make-up. Blusher, pale powder, eyeliner, and deep red lipstick all became very popular in the 1920s.

Did you know?

The name "it girl" came from a 1927 film called *It*. The film starred Clara Bow as a young shop assistant who was determined to have fun. In the film, "it" referred to Bow's sex appeal. Bow became known as the it girl and was a role model for young women around the world.[1]

Quote

"She is, frankly, heavily made up … poisonously scarlet lips, richly ringed eyes … Her skirt comes just an inch below her knees, overlapping by a faint fraction her rolled and twisted stockings. The idea is that when she walks in a bit of a breeze, you shall now and then observe the knee … She wears of course the newest thing in bobs."

A magazine article from 1925, describing "Flapper Jane"[2]

Fashions for men

In the 1920s, young men began to abandon the stiff, formal clothes worn by their fathers. They wore loose-fitting suits, sweaters, striped blazers in summer, and Oxford bags, which were wide, loose trousers. Fashionable men often wore two-tone shoes in the day, and shiny, patent leather shoes at night. Hair was greased down and parted in the middle. Flat caps and straw **boaters** were very fashionable in the 1920s.

Fashions of the 1930s

Women's fashions changed in the 1930s. Skirts became fuller and longer, reaching to mid-calf, and the waist and bust were emphasized. Backless dresses were very popular for evening wear. Some daring women sported leisure wear, which consisted of wide pyjama-style trousers with a short jacket. Fashionable men wore double-breasted suits with padded shoulders. Their suits were usually made from a dark, pinstriped material, and had wide trouser legs. For their leisure activities, men wore knickerbockers and woollen sweaters with Scottish patterns.

Gangster style

Most people could not afford new clothes during the years of the Great Depression. However, one group in the United States with plenty of money were the bootleggers – the gangsters who had grown rich by smuggling alcohol. Gangsters wore an exaggerated version of the double-breasted suit, with broader shoulders, narrower waists, and wider trouser bottoms. They chose colourful ties and finished off the look with a wide-brimmed, soft felt hat. This extreme gangster style was laughed at by members of the older generation, but it was copied by some fashionable young men.

Fashion icons

In the 1930s, fashionable men and women started to base their style on the film stars of Hollywood, who were the fashion icons of the day. Men also copied the clothes of the British Prince of Wales, who was later known as the Duke of Windsor. Men wore jackets and trousers with a "Prince of Wales check". This was a Scottish design of large and small checks, also called glen plaid. The prince's double-breasted Windsor suits were copied as well. The Duke of Windsor's wife, Wallis Simpson, was also a leading fashion icon in the 1930s.[3]

The Duke and Duchess of Windsor in 1939. Even when they were casually dressed, the couple still had a great sense of style.

A royal drama

In the mid-1930s, people all over the world were fascinated by the story of a very glamorous couple: the Prince of Wales, who was **heir** to the British throne, and Wallis Simpson. Wallis Simpson had been divorced twice so she could not be accepted as the British queen. In 1936, King George V died and the Prince of Wales became King Edward VIII. He soon realized that he was faced with a terrible choice. He could either remain king and give up Wallis Simpson, or marry Wallis and give up the crown. Before his **coronation**, he decided to give up the throne, or **abdicate**. His younger brother became the new king and Edward was given the title of the Duke of Windsor. He married Wallis Simpson and the couple spent most of their life in France.[4]

Marathons

During the 1920s, a craze for **marathons** swept through the United States. Young people competed against each other to see who could last the longest in non-stop contests for kissing, talking, laughing, eating, or drinking. Some people even held competitions for non-stop rocking in a rocking chair.

Dance marathons were especially popular. They were held in towns and cities all over the United States, and couples competed for prize money by dancing almost non-stop for hundreds of hours. Contestants had to remain in motion for 45 minutes each hour, 24 hours a day. Some dancers had trays hanging from their necks so they could eat meals or write letters while they danced. To help pass the time, they read newspapers or books, knitted or sewed, and even fell asleep while their partner supported their weight!

Pulling stunts

Another craze of the 1920s was called pulling **stunts**. This involved performing daring acts in front of large crowds. The stunts were often extremely dangerous. Some daredevils were shot from a cannon, sat on top of a flag pole, or walked on stilts on the ledges of high buildings.

Dance marathons were true tests of endurance. One man dropped dead on the dance floor after 87 hours of non-stop dancing in a dance marathon.

Barnstormers and wing walkers

The most amazing stunts involved small planes. Daredevil pilots performed spectacular moves such as barrel rolls, which is when a plane rolls over and back up again in mid-air. Pilots also wowed viewers by flying very low. They were known as barnstormers because they sometimes flew right through the open doors of a barn.

Wing walkers walked on the wings of planes while they were in flight. Some even did handstands, danced, or played tennis on the wings of planes. Another popular stunt was hopping from one plane to another, or from a car, a boat, or a train on to the wing of a plane. Flying circuses performed a range of stunts in front of huge crowds, but most of these circuses failed after the Great Depression began.

Charles Lindbergh (1902-1974)

Charles Lindbergh spent most of his childhood in Minnesota. He was fascinated by flying, and by the age of 20 he was working as a wing walker. He made his first solo flight when he was 21, and went on to be a barnstorming pilot known as Daredevil Lindbergh. In 1927, at the age of 25, he became world famous as the first man to fly across the Atlantic Ocean alone. His solo, non-stop flight from New York to Paris took 33.5 hours and covered 5,600 kilometres (3,500 miles). In later life, Lindbergh was an author, an explorer, and an inventor.[5] He also became known for expressing his social views, many of which were controversial and even racist.

Did you know?

The popular dance called the Lindy Hop (see page 13) was named after Charles Lindbergh. After Lindbergh's famous flight to Paris, one newspaper headline read: "Lindy hops the Atlantic". Very soon people were dancing the Lindy Hop, which involved spectacular jumps into the air.[6]

Bicycles, motorcycles, and cars

In the 1920s, many people took up cycling and motoring. Young people joined cycling clubs to explore the countryside. Dashing young men, and a few young women, rode motorcycles, and the roads began to fill up with automobiles. Cars were cheaper than they had been before World War I, but they were still an exciting novelty. Some wealthy girls drove their own cars. They were considered shockingly independent by the older generation.

Sports

Sports flourished in the years between World War I and World War II. In particular, women began to take part in more vigorous outdoor sports. The increased public interest in sports was partly due to live radio broadcasts of matches and tournaments. Golf, tennis, boxing, football, and baseball were especially popular. Football in the United Kingdom and baseball in the United States became major spectator sports, and the stars of the games were household names.

The game of miniature golf was created in the United States in 1922, and immediately set off a craze in America and Europe. Soon there were over 150 rooftop courses in New York City and tens of thousands across the United States. The boom in miniature golf did not survive the Great Depression. Nearly all the American courses closed in the 1930s.[7]

Some people with cars enjoyed driving to country sports events. This wealthy family is watching a horse race.

Did you know?

Pogo sticks were a major craze in the early 1920s. They became even more popular after the dancers at the Ziegfeld Follies, a New York variety show (see page 16), learned how to pogo. Sometimes a whole show was performed on pogo sticks. In one famous show, the Ziegfeld dancers managed to bounce their way through a mock wedding![8]

The craze for pogo sticks led to some very surprising sights. This girl is combining jumping on her pogo stick with taking her dog for a walk.

Games and toys

In the early 1920s, a craze for the Chinese game of mahjong swept through the British Empire, Europe, North America, and Japan.[9] Mahjong is usually played by four people, using a set of tiles with Chinese characters and symbols.

Crosswords had been invented in 1913, but it was not until the mid-1920s that the crossword craze really took off.[10] Most leading newspapers had a daily crossword puzzle, and the puzzles were so popular that several songs were written about them. The songs had humorous titles such as "Cross Words Between Sweetie and Me" and "Cross Word Puzzle Blues".

The board game *Monopoly* was widely launched in America in 1935 and was an instant hit. People enjoyed the "real-life" excitement of the game, which was based on buying and selling land and building on the properties. It appeared in the United Kingdom in 1936, and within two years versions were being sold in Australia and all over Europe.[11]

In 1928, the world's first yo-yo factory was opened in California. Four years later the company was bought by a businessman named Donald Duncan, who made the yo-yo famous all over the world. Duncan organized yo-yo contests that were promoted by newspapers across the United States.[12]

Changing times

The outbreak of war in Europe in 1939 changed popular culture. In less than 12 months, many European film and theatre stars had joined the armed forces. A few went to fight, but most of them became entertainers for the troops. In 1941, when the United States joined the war, a stream of actors, entertainers, and musicians left America. During the war years, people still enjoyed films, theatre, music, and radio, but much of the glamour had disappeared from these industries.

A changing society

By the end of the 1930s, some major changes had taken place in society, and these changes were clearly expressed in popular culture. In the years between World War I and World War II the younger generation developed its own youth culture and began to lead the way in music and fashion.

African Americans played a very important role in the cultural life of the period. Jazz had its origins in the music of African Americans, and early stars of jazz, blues, and swing were black. Black musicians and singers were widely admired, but sadly this did not change the way most African Americans were treated. In many parts of America they still had to live as second-class citizens.

By the 1930s, the **cult** of the celebrity had really taken off in the worlds of film, music, and sport. The first major film stars emerged at this time, and celebrity magazines kept people informed about the stars' romances and the fashions they wore. Many of the early film celebrities were female. Strong, confident women such as Mae West, Josephine Baker, and Katharine Hepburn provided a new kind of role model for women.

Shared entertainment

Cinema and radio had the effect of bringing people closer together. People who lived thousands of kilometres apart could see the same films and listen to the same radio programmes. When the BBC launched its Empire Service in 1932, listeners all over the world tuned in to the same programmes. The sense of togetherness created by the radio was especially important during World War II.

Not forgotten

Some elements of popular culture from the 1920s and 1930s have lasted right up to the present day. We still listen to jazz and blues songs that were written 90 years ago. We enjoy the art and literature of the period, and we still watch the great film classics, such as *The Wizard of Oz*. Today people look back on the years between World War I and World War II as a golden age for popular culture.

The most significant event in popular culture between World War I and World War II was the birth of jazz. It is not surprising that this period is sometimes known as the Jazz Age.

Timeline

1918
World War I ends

1919
Joe Oliver and his band move from New Orleans to Chicago. This marks the start of the spread of jazz.

1920
The US government passes the Prohibition law, banning the making and sale of alcohol

The first commercial radio station in the United States is set up

1921
Charlie Chaplin and Jackie Coogan star in the silent film *The Kid*

1922
Archaeologist Howard Carter discovers the tomb of Tutankhamen

1923
Jelly Roll Morton and his band move from New Orleans to Chicago

Walt Disney starts to make animated films

1924
George Gershwin writes "Rhapsody in Blue", combining classical music with jazz

1925
F. Scott Fitzgerald publishes *The Great Gatsby*, his novel expressing the spirit of the Jazz Age

1926
The magazine *Amazing Stories* is launched in the United States to publish science fiction stories

1927
Charles Lindbergh is the first man to fly a plane across the Atlantic Ocean alone

1928
Amelia Earhart is the first woman to fly a plane across the Atlantic Ocean alone

1929
The Wall Street Crash (a major financial collapse in America) results in the Great Depression, which affects countries worldwide

1930
The Chrysler Building in New York is completed. It is the tallest building in the world.

1931
The Empire State Building in New York is completed. It replaces the Chrysler Building as the world's tallest building.

Two classic horror films, *Dracula* and *Frankenstein*, are released

1933
Adolf Hitler becomes chancellor of Germany

Prohibition in the United States ends

President Roosevelt launches the New Deal, a campaign to improve the lives of Americans who had been severely hit by the Great Depression

1934
Bonnie Parker and Clyde Barrow are captured and shot

Technicolor introduces "glorious Technicolor," a new kind of colour film

1935
Fred Astaire and Ginger Rogers star in the film *Top Hat*

1936
Margaret Mitchell's best-selling novel *Gone With the Wind* is published

Regular TV broadcasts begin in the United Kingdom

1938
Hitler and the Nazi party start a major persecution campaign against the Jews in Germany, and Hitler invades Austria

Action Comics 1 includes the first appearance of Superman

J. R. R. Tolkien publishes his first children's book, *The Hobbit*

Regular TV broadcasts begin in the United States

1939
Hitler invades Poland, and World War II begins in Europe

The films *The Wizard of Oz* and *Gone With the Wind* are released

John Steinbeck publishes *The Grapes of Wrath*, his powerful novel about the Great Depression

Best of the era

The best way to find out about the pop culture of the 1920s and 1930s is to experience it for yourself. Here are some suggestions for the best or most typical examples that will give you a sense of the time:

Films

The Kid (1921) (silent comedy, starring Charlie Chaplin)
Battleship Potemkin (1925) (silent historical drama)
The Jazz Singer (1927) (the first talkie)
Dracula (1931) (horror film)
Frankenstein (1931) (horror film)
Queen Christina (1933) (historical drama, starring Greta Garbo)
King Kong (1933) (adventure, starring Fay Wray)
A Night at the Opera (1935) (comedy, starring the Marx Brothers)
Mutiny on the Bounty (1935) (adventure, starring Charles Laughton)
Modern Times (1936) (comedy, starring Charlie Chaplin)
Snow White and the Seven Dwarfs (1937) (Walt Disney cartoon)
Bringing Up Baby (1938) (screwball comedy)
Stagecoach (1939) (western, starring John Wayne)
The Wizard of Oz (1939) (fantasy, starring Judy Garland)

Music

"Tea for Two" (1925, Vincent Youmans and Irving Caesar)
"I Got Rhythm" (1930, George and Ira Gershwin)
"Mad Dogs and Englishmen" (1931, Noël Coward)
"Anything Goes" (1934, Cole Porter)
"Blue Moon" (1934, Richard Rodgers and Lorenz Hart)

Architecture

Empire State Building, New York (1930–1931)
Chrysler Building, New York (1930–1931)
Board of Trade Building, Chicago (1930)

Books

Women in Love (1920): D. H. Lawrence
A Farewell to Arms (1929): Ernest Hemingway
Murder on the Orient Express (1934): Agatha Christie
The Nine Tailors (1934): Dorothy L. Sayers
Gone With the Wind (1936): Margaret Mitchell
Brighton Rock (1938): Graham Greene
The Grapes of Wrath (1939): John Steinbeck
The Big Sleep (1939): Raymond Chandler

Notes on sources

What is popular culture?

1. "Prohibition," *Spartacus Educational*, http://www.spartacus.schoolnet.co.uk/USAprohibition.htm, Accessed July 14, 2011.

2. Jennifer Rosenberg, "The Great Depression," *About.com*, http://history1900s.about.com/od/1930s/p/greatdepression.htm, Accessed July 14, 2011.

3. "Adolf Hitler," *History Learning Site*, http://www.historylearningsite.co.uk/adolf_hitler.htm, Accessed July 14, 2011.

4. "Joseph Stalin," *Spartacus Educational*, http://www.spartacus.schoolnet.co.uk/RUSstalin.htm, Accessed on 14 July 2011

5. Jennifer Rosenberg, "Bonnie and Clyde," *About.com*, http://history1900s.about.com/od/1930s/a/bonnieandclyde.htm, Accessed July 14, 2011.

Jazz, blues, and swing

1. "Jelly Roll Morton: Biography," *Classical Cat*, http://classicalcat.opusfinder.com/morton_jr/biography.php?lang=nl, Accessed June 14, 2011.

2. "Louis (Satchmo) Armstrong (1901–1971)," *The Red Hot Jazz Archive*, http://www.redhotjazz.com/louie.html, Accessed June 14, 2011.

3. "Jelly Roll Morton: Biography," *Classical Cat*.

4 "Louis (Satchmo) Armstrong (1901–1971)," *The Red Hot Jazz Archive*.

5. "Charleston," *Columbia Electronic Encyclopedia*, http://www.infoplease.com/ce6/ent/A0811494.html, Accessed June 14, 2011.

6. "Mamie Smith (1883–1946)," *The Red Hot Jazz Archive*, http://www.redhotjazz.com/mamie.html, Accessed June 14, 2011.

7. "Ma Rainey: Biography," bio.true story, http://www.biography.com/articles/Ma-Rainey-9542413?part=0, Accessed June 14, 2011.

8. "Bessie Smith: Biography," *bio.true story*, http://www.biography.com/articles/Bessie-Smith-9486520, Accessed June 14, 2011.

9. Randall Stross, "Edison the Inventor, Edison the Showman," *New York Times*, March 11, 2007, http://query.nytimes.com/gst/fullpage.html?res=9B03E5DC1331F932A25750C0A9619C8B63&pagewanted=1, Accessed July 14, 2011; "The Devil's Music: 1920s Jazz," Culture Shock: The TV Series and Beyond, PBS.org, http://www.pbs.org/wgbh/cultureshock/beyond/jazz.html, Accessed July 14, 2011.

10. "Duke Ellington: Biography,", *bio.true story*, http://www.biography.com/articles/Duke-Ellington-9286338, Accessed June 14, 2011.

11. "Nov 21, 1934: Ella Fitzgerald Wins Amateur Night at Harlem's Apollo Theater," This Day in History, *History.com*, http://www.history.com/this-day-in-history/ella-fitzgerald-wins-amateur-night-at-harlem39s-apollo-theater, Accessed June 14, 2011.

12. "Cotton Club," *Encyclopedia of the Harlem Renaissance*, http://cw.routledge.com/ref/harlem/cotton.html, Accessed July 14, 2011.

13. Petri Liukkonen, "Langston Hughes (1902–1967)," *Authors' Calendar*, http://www.kirjasto.sci.fi/lhughes.htm, Accessed June 14, 2011.

14. Jone Johnson Lewis, "Zora Neale Hurston," *About.com* Guide, http://womenshistory.about.com/od/hurstonzoraneale/p/hurston_bio.htm, Accessed June 14, 2011.

Vaudeville, musicals, and dance

1. "Ziegfeld 101," *Musicals 101*, http://www.musicals101.com/ziegfeld.htm, Accessed June 14, 2011.

2. John Kenrick, "A History of the Musical Minstrel Shows," *Musicals 101*, http://www.musicals101.com/minstrel.htm, Accessed July 14, 2011;

"The Minstrel Show," George Mason University|Centre for History and New Media, http://chnm.gmu.edu/courses/jackson/minstrel/minstrel.html, Accessed July 14, 2011.

3. "Josephine Baker Biography," *Encyclopedia of World Biography*, http://www.notablebiographies.com/Ba-Be/Baker-Josephine.html, Accessed June 14, 2011.

4. John Kenrick, "A History of Cabaret," *Musicals 101*, http://www.musicals101.com/cabaret.htm, Accessed June 14, 2011.

5. "George Gershwin: Biography," *bio.true story*, http://www.biography.com/articles/George-Gershwin-9309643, Accessed June 14, 2011.

6. "Sir Noël Coward: Biography," *bio.true story*, http://www.biography.com/articles/Sir-Noel-Coward-9259629, Accessed July 15, 2011.

7. John Kenrick, "RKO: Fred and Ginger," History of Musical Film 1930s, *Musicals 101*, http://www.musicals101.com/1930film3.htm, Accessed June 14, 2011.

8. "Fred Astaire: Biography," *bio.true story*, http://www.biography.com/articles/Fred-Astaire-9190991?part=0, Accessed June 14, 2011.

Fantastic films

1. Robert E. Yahnke, "Films From the Silent Era," Cinema History, http://www.tc.umn.edu/~ryahnke/film/cinema1.htm, Accessed June 14, 2011.

2. "Buster Keaton: Biography," *bio.true story*, http://www.biography.com/articles/Buster-Keaton-9361442, Accessed June 14, 2011.

3. "Sergey Eisenstein: Biography," *bio.true story*, http://www.biography.com/articles/Sergey-Eisenstein-40942, Accessed July 15, 2011.

4. "Charlie Chaplin: Biography," *bio.true story*, http://www.biography.com/featured-biography/charlie-chaplin/, Accessed June 14, 2011.

5. Jeffrey Dym, "A Brief History of Benshi," *About Japan*, http://aboutjapan.japansociety.org/content.cfm/a_brief_history_of_benshi, Accessed June 14, 2011.

6. "The Jazz Singer," *answers.com*, http://www.answers.com/topic/the-jazz-singer, Accessed June 14, 2011.

7. "The Marx Brothers: Movies," *The Marx Brothers*, http://www.marx-brothers.org/watching/movies.htm, Accessed June 14, 2011.

8. "Charlie Chaplin: Biography," *bio.true story*.

9. "A short history of Hollywood," *HistoricLA.com*, http://www.historicla.com/hollywood/history.html, Accessed June 14, 2011.

10. "1930s'Hollywood Opens the Door to the Golden Era," *Hollywood moviememories.com*, http://www.hollywoodmoviememories.com/articles/hollywood-history/1930s-hollywood-opens-door-golden.php, Accessed June 14, 2011.

11. "The First Horror Movies," *Horror Film History*, http://www.horrorfilmhistory.com/index.php?pageID=1920s, Accessed June 14, 2011.

12. "Horror Begins To Talk... and Scream," *Horror Film History*, http://www.horrorfilmhistory.com/index.php?pageID=1930s, Accessed June 14, 2011.

13. "Horror Begins To Talk... and Scream," *Horror Film History*.

14. Ray Morton, King Kong: *The History of a Movie Icon From Fay Wray to Peter Jackson* (New York: Applause Theatre & Cinema Books, 2005).

15. Morton, *King Kong*, 33-36.

16. Tim Dirks, "Little Caesar (1930)," *filmsite*, http://www.filmsite.org/littc.html, Accessed June 14, 2011.

17. Tim Dirks, "The Public Enemy (1931)," *filmsite*, http://www.filmsite.org/publ.html, Accessed June 14, 2011.

18. Doug Warren and James Cagney, *Cagney: The Authorized Biography* (New York: Mass Market ed., 1986, 90).

19. "Glorious Technicolor 1932–1955," *The American Widescreen Museum*, http://www.widescreenmuseum.com/oldcolor/technicolor4.htm, Accessed June 14, 2011.

19. Tim Dirks, "The Golden Age of Hollywood: From 1930 to 1948," http://www.filmsite.org/30sintro.html, Accessed 8/16/2011.

20. "Fred Astaire: Biography," *bio.true story*.

22. "Film History Milestones: 1933," *filmsite*, http://www.filmsite.org/1933-filmhistory.html, Accessed June 14, 2011.

23. "Company History," *The Walt Disney Company*, http://corporate.disney.go.com/corporate/complete_history_1.html, Accessed June 14, 2011.

24. "Company History," *The Walt Disney Company*.

25. "1939 Academy Awards," *filmsite*, http://www.filmsite.org/aa39.html, Accessed June 14, 2011.

The Golden Age of Radio

1. Mary Bellis, "The History of Radio," *About.com. Inventors*, http://inventors.about.com/od/rstartinventions/a/radio_2.htm, Accessed June 14, 2011.

2. "The History and Development of Radio in the UK," *MediaUK*, http://www.mediauk.com/article/20411/the-history-and-development-of-radio-in-the-uk, Accessed June 14, 2011.

3. Asa Briggs, *History of Broadcasting in the UK*, Vol.1 (Oxford: Oxford University Press, 1961), 258.

4. "NBC Symphony Orchestra," *allmusic*, http://www.allmusic.com/artist/nbc-symphony-orchestra-p359992, Accessed June 14, 2011; "1930s Innovations," The BBC Story, http://www.bbc.co.uk/historyofthebbc/innovation/30s_printable.shtml, Accessed June 14, 2011.

5. "History of the Opry," *Grand Ole Opry*, http://www.opry.com/about/History.html, Accessed June 14, 2011.

6. Asa Briggs, *History of Broadcasting*, 75.

7. "Gertrude Berg (1899–1966)," *Jewish Virtual Library*, http://www.jewishvirtuallibrary.org/jsource/biography/berg.html, Accessed June 14, 2011.

8. "War of the Worlds Radio Broadcast (1938)," *War of the Worlds*, http://www.war-ofthe-worlds.co.uk/war_worlds_orson_welles_mercury.htm, Accessed June 14, 2011.

9. Asa Briggs, *History of Broadcasting*, 260-62.

10. "The History of the BBC: The First TV Era," *Telectronic: The Television History Site*, http://www.teletronic.co.uk/tvera.htm, Accessed June 14, 2011; Mitchell Stephens, "History of Television," http://www.nyu.edu/classes/stephens/History%20of%20Television%20page.htm, Accessed June 14, 2011.

11. "1920s Innovations," *The BBC Story*, http://www.bbc.co.uk/historyofthebbc/innovation/20s_printable.shtml, Accessed June 14, 2011.

Books, magazines, and comics

1. "About Gone With the Wind," *Margaret Mitchell House*, http://www.atlantahistorycenter.com/cms/About+Gone+With+the+Wind+/239.html, Accessed June 14, 2011.

2. "About Penguin: Company History," *Penguin Books*, http://www.penguin.co.uk/static/cs/uk/0/aboutus/aboutpenguin_companyhistory.html, Accessed June 14, 2011.

3. "Science Fiction Gets a Home," History of the Pulps, *Pulpworld*, http://www.pulpworld.com/history/history_02.htm, Accessed June 14, 2011.

4. "Superman Comics History," *Superman Homepage*, http://www.supermanhomepage.com/comics/comics.php?topic=comics-history, Accessed June 14, 2011.

5. "Hergé: Key Dates and Milestones," *Tintin.com*, http://www.tintin.com/uk/#/tintin/essentiel/essentiel.swf?page=1, Accessed June 14, 2011.

Architecture, design, and the visual arts

1. Heather Cross, "What Kind of Art and Architecture Are in the Chrysler Building?", *About.com*, http://gonyc.about.com/od/tipsforvisitingnyc/f/Chrysler-Building-Art.htm, Accessed June 14, 2011.

2. Jennifer Rosenberg, "The Empire State Building," *About.com*, http://history1900s.about.com/od/1930s/a/empirestatebldg.htm, Accessed June 14, 2011.

3. "History of American Art Deco," *Bryn Mawr College*, http://www.brynmawr.edu/cities/archx/05-600/proj/p2/npk/historydeco.htm, Accessed July 15, 2011; "Art Deco 1910–1939," Victoria and Albert Museum, www.vam.ac.uk/vastatic/microsites/1157_art_deco/, Accessed July 15, 2011;

"Homes: Art Deco," BBC Homes, http://www.bbc.co.uk/homes/design/period_artdeco.shtml, Accessed July 15, 2011.

4. Jennifer Rosenberg, "Tomb of King Tut Found!", *About.com*, http://history1900s.about.com/od/1920s/a/kingtut.htm, Accessed June 14, 2011.

Fashions, stunts, and crazes

1. "Clara Bow: Biography," *bio.true story*, http://www.biography.com/articles/Clara-Bow-9221851, Accessed July 15, 2011.

2. Bruce Bliven, "Flapper Jane," reprinted from *New Republic*, 1925, www.colorado.edu/AmStudies/lewis/1025/flapperjane.pdf, Accessed June 14, 2011.

3. "Style Profile—Duke of Windsor," *Dandy Fashioner*, http://dandyfashioner.blogspot.com/2009/10/style-profile-duke-of-windsor.html, Accessed July 15, 2011.

4. Jennifer Rosenberg, "King Edward VIII Abdicated for Love," *About.com*, http://history1900s.about.com/od/1930s/a/kingedward.htm, Accessed June 14, 2011.

5. "Charles Lindbergh: Biography," *bio.truestory*, http://www.biography.com/articles/Charles-Lindbergh-9382609, Accessed June 14, 2011.

6. "What Is Lindy Hop?", dancing.org, http://dancing.org/lindy-what-is.html, Accessed June 14, 2011.

7. Mary Bellis, "The History of Miniature Golf," *About.com*, http://inventors.about.com/od/mstartinventions/a/minature_golf.htm, Accessed June 14, 2011.

8. Mary Bellis, "Pogo Stick," *About.com*, http://inventors.about.com/library/inventors/bl_pogo_stick.htm, Accessed June 14, 2011.

9. "Mahjong: An Introduction Into the Western World," *MahJongDragon*, http://www.mahjongdragon.com/mahjong-west.php, Accessed June 14, 2011.

10. "Fads, Fashions, & American Influences," *historyclass*, http://historyclass.tripod.com/id5.html, Accessed June 14, 2011.

11. "Monopoly Game history," *MonopolyCity.com*, http://www.monopolycity.com/ac_monopoly_history.html, Accessed June 14, 2011.

12. Mary Bellis, "The History of the YoYo," *About.com*, http://inventors.about.com/od/xyzstartinventions/a/yoyo.htm, Accessed June 14, 2011.

Find out more

Books

America in the 1920s (Decades of Twentieth-Century America), Edmund Lindop and Margaret J. Goldstein (Twenty First Century Books, 2009)

From Speakeasies to Stalinism: The Early 1920s to the Mid 1930s (Modern Eras Uncovered), Patricia Levy (Raintree, 2006)

How Did It Happen? The Rise of Nazism, Charles Freeman (Franklin Watts, 2007)

The Grapes of Wrath, John Steinbeck (Penguin Modern Classics, 2000)

The Great Gatsby, F. Scott Fitzgerald (Penguin Modern Classics, 2000)

Websites

www.1920-30.com
A general site on the Roaring Twenties. Includes sections on architecture, music, dance, toys, and sports.

www.fashion-era.com/1920s/index.htm
Describes and illustrates fashions of the 1920s.

www.fashion-era.com/1930s/index.htm
Describes and illustrates fashions of the 1930s.

www.filmsite.org/20sintro.html
A history of film in the 1920s.

www.filmsite.org/30sintro.html
A history of film in the 1930s.

www.vam.ac.uk/vastatic/microsites/1157_art_deco
A site on art deco style from the Victoria and Albert Museum in London.

Places to visit

Fashion and design in the 1920s and 1930s:
Design Museum, London
National Design Museum, New York
Victoria and Albert Museum, London

The history of jazz:
Jazz Museum, Harlem, New York

Films in the 1920s and 1930s:
Hollywood Museum, Los Angeles
Museum of the Moving Image, Bradford, Yorkshire, UK
Museum of the Moving Image, London
Museum of the Moving Image, New York

Topics for further research

• Research the history of jazz and blues.

• Read more about the fashions of the 1920s and 1930s.

• Explore the world of Art Deco style (in architecture, interior design, household items, or jewellery).

Glossary

abdicate act of a monarch giving up his or her throne

animated (films) films that are made by taking millions of shots of drawings or models and then putting all the shots together

archaeologist someone who uncovers objects or buildings in order to find out more about the past

aristocrat member of the upper class

art deco style that was very popular in the 1920s and 1930s for buildings and furniture. Art deco designs have sharp, clear outlines and use geometric shapes, such as triangles.

assembly line moving belt in a factory that carries parts that are put together to make a product

bawdy humorously indecent

blues type of music that was created by African American slaves. Blues music is sad but powerful and has a very strong rhythm.

boater circular straw hat with a flat top and a wide brim

Broadway a street in New York that has all the main theatres

butler personal servant to the very rich. A butler serves drinks and helps to organize his master and mistress's life.

chrome very shiny silver-coloured metal

colony foreign country, or part of a foreign country, that has been taken over and controlled by another nation

communism form of government in which the state owns all the land and factories and provides for people's needs

consumer goods products bought and used by average people

coronation ceremony of the crowning of a king or queen

cult movement with many ardent followers

department store very large shop with many departments

dialogue words spoken by actors in films or plays

economy wealth created by businesses, factories, farming, etc.

episode one performance that is part of a long-running series

exotic strange and glamorous; from a foreign country

French resistance secret movement formed in France during World War II with the aim of weakening the Nazis' control over France

gramophone machine for playing music records

Great Depression period lasting from 1929 until the late 1930s, when countries in many parts of the world had serious financial problems and their banks and businesses lost lots of money

heir someone who inherits a title or money from one or both parents

immigrant person who comes from another country to settle in a new country

improvise make up or invent at the time of a performance

marathon competition or test to see how long people can keep doing the same thing

minor key music in a minor key sounds sad. Piano music in a minor key uses lots of black keys.

minstrel song song sung by white musicians, with their faces painted black, who are pretending to be African American. Minstrel songs are often accompanied by a banjo.

mock-Tudor a style of architecture that mimics Tudor buildings, with dark beams and small window panes

moral having to do with the principles of right and wrong

on location (filming) in a real place, not in a studio

persecute treat very cruelly

Prohibition law passed in 1920 by the US government that banned the making and sale of alcohol. Prohibition lasted until 1933.

release (film or music) make available to the public as a film or a recording

sequel second film or book that features some of the same characters as the first one

serial (radio) long-running series of programmes

sheet music music printed on sheets of paper so that people can play it

soloist player of a musical instrument, who often plays alone

speakeasy illegal bar that was popular in the United States in the 1920s and early 1930s

special effects sounds, models, and images specially created for film, theatre, TV, or radio to make people believe that what they are seeing is real

stunt very daring act that is often performed in front of a crowd

supplement something that is provided as an extra

surrealism style of art in which artists create strange, dreamlike pictures

swing (music) type of music that is similar to jazz, which has a fast rhythm and is very easy to dance to. Swing music is played by big bands.

talkies films with a soundtrack

variety show show that includes acts by musicians, dancers, singers, and comedians

vaudeville show that includes acts by musicians, dancers, singers, and comedians. Vaudeville is another name for a variety show and was called music hall in the United Kingdom.

Index